Discovery Girls' Guide to...

Growing Up

Everything You Need to Know
About Your Changing Body

From the creators of *Discovery Girls* magazine,
winner of the Mom's Choice Award, NAPPA Silver Award,
iParenting Media Award, and Parents' Choice Award.

Discovery Girls, Inc.
CALIFORNIA

Discovery Girls, Inc.
445 South San Antonio Rd, Ste. 205
Los Altos, California 94022

Discovery Girls' Guide to Growing Up:
Everything You Need to Know About Your Changing Body

Copyright © 2013 Discovery Girls, Inc.

By the editors of *Discovery Girls* magazine.

Illustrations by Aruna Rangarajan.

The advice in this book is not intended to replace that of girls' parents, physicians, psychologists, teachers, or other experts. It should be used as an additional resource only. Questions and concerns about mental or physical health should be discussed with a doctor or qualified healthcare professional.

Many people contributed to the design and writing of this book, which was five years in the making. It was a labor of love for the Discovery Girls creative team, and the passion and enthusiasm of everyone involved can be seen in every page of the final product. The Discovery Girls creative team consists of: Catherine Lee, Founder and CEO; Sarah Verney, Editorial Director; Gloria Jeong, Associate Art Director; Linda Stewart, Content Manager; Holly Hanbury-Brown, Associate Web Editor; Roberta Hall and Zhiya Zhu, Graphic Designers; and Shirley Patino, Circulation Manager. In addition, significant contributions were made by writer/editor Marina Khidekel and former Discovery Girls interns Lyn Me'heula and Olivia Tran. Forgive us for not mentioning the many other people who contributed creative ideas and support throughout those five years. You are too numerous to list, but you have our eternal gratitude.

All statistics and quotes in this book, unless otherwise noted, were collected via online surveys of readers of *Discovery Girls* magazine conducted by Discovery Girls, Inc. from 2011 to 2013. Because the surveys were done anonymously, no girls' names have been used with the quotes.

ISBN 978-1-934766-16-3

Visit Discovery Girls' web site at www.DiscoveryGirls.com.
Printed in South Korea.

Acknowledgments

I'd like to send a special thank you to all of the amazing girls who have read *Discovery Girls* magazine over the years and have generously shared your thoughts and ideas with us.

Special Thanks to Our Discovery Girls

I would also like to thank and acknowledge these Discovery Girls for acting as our young editorial board. Their suggestions helped keep the book real and relevant.

Abigail, age 11, Ontario
Abygail, age 11, MI
Amanda, age 12, CA
Ava, age 10, Ontario
Brittany, age 11, NJ
Cassie, age 12, IL
Catarina, age 11, TX
Cindy, age 12, Ontario
Elizabeth, age 9, CA
Emilee, age 11, CA
Emily, age 9, British Columbia
Gabby, age 11, FL
Gabrielle, age 11, OR
Gracie, age 10, GA
Hailey, age 11, IL
Isabella, age 12, CA
Karolina, age 12, CA
Katie, age 9, FL

Katie, age 9, MO
Layla, age 11, WI
Madison, age 11, ME
Marielle, age 11, PA
Marika, age 12, Nova Scotia
Mary Claire, age 13, IN
Maya, age 9, MA
Mia, age 13, MO
Morgan, age 10, VA
Rachel, age 11, MO
Rebecca, age 12, NY
Ros, age 12, WA
Sabrina, age 11, OR
Sara, age 12, WA
Sequoya, age 11, CA
Siena, age 12, OR
Vanessa, age 10, Ontario

Thanks to Our Discovery Girls' Mothers

Finally, I'd like to thank these girls' mothers for their generous support, careful reading, and suggestions, and send an *extra* special thank you to the following moms for going above and beyond: Bonnie Prokopowicz, Carolyn Lewis, Carolynne Yen, Catherine Dumas, Christine Du Bois-Buxbaum, Elizabeth Du Vinage, Lori Morin, Luanne Schenkels, Phyllis Milton, Rae Bullard, Shawnda Walker, Valerie Hamaker, and Wendy Luu.

Catherine Lee
PUBLISHER
DISCOVERY GIRLS, INC.

Contents

1

Your Changing Body

Puberty & You

Puberty is an exciting time, but it can be frustrating, too. You're not a little kid anymore, but you're not an adult either. You're **caught somewhere in between.**

Your body is changing and sometimes your emotions feel like they're going crazy. Maybe your clothes don't fit right anymore, or you don't feel comfortable in your own body, or you start crying just because your mom asks you to clean up your room. No wonder you sometimes feel confused!

But here's the thing about puberty: everyone goes through it. From the most popular girl at school to the boy you have a crush on, to your favorite celebrity! Even your parents went through puberty once...so you can take comfort in the fact that the things that are happening to you happen to everyone else, too!

56% of girls learn the **most about puberty from their moms**.

"I feel like I am the only person going through the changes and *everyone else is perfectly normal* when I'm not."

"I am a little scared to wake up one morning and look in the mirror and *find a different me.*"

"I feel like sometimes *no one understands* me."

"I like getting older and maturing. *I feel special,* like I'm joining a 'teenagers' club' or something."

"I'm annoyed. *Everything starts changing* and doesn't stop. New changes just keep coming. Once you get used to one change, along comes a new one."

"*I feel a little unsure at times.* I am constantly wondering if other girls are going through the same thing or if I am different."

WHAT'S HAPPENING to me?

If your body has started changing, you've probably noticed that a few things are different. Here's some basic information about what your body is going through (or will go through very soon!).

1. You're getting taller.

You've always been growing, but now it seems like you're growing literally overnight. **You'll probably have a growth spurt or two,** which is when you grow a lot in a short period of time. Feeling taller than you were just a week ago? That's totally normal!

You've probably also noticed that you're a lot taller than the boys in your grade. (This can make things like slow dancing awkward!) Boys generally don't hit puberty until a couple of years after girls do. This means girls are usually more mature, too. You may roll your eyes when all the boys in your grade still laugh at potty jokes, but that's the way things happen. You should just feel good that you're growing up—they'll catch up, eventually.

10.5
is the average **age girls start puberty.***

2. Your feet are getting bigger.

Just like a taller tree needs bigger roots to keep it standing straight, your body needs bigger feet to stay balanced when you're growing. Imagine trying to balance your new, taller body on tiny feet! You'd look ridiculous!

> *Last summer, my feet wouldn't stop growing! In May I was a size six, and by the time school started, I was a size nine. My mom and I had to go shoe shopping all the time!*

*Source: DukeHealth.org

"My mother saw the **hair under my arms** and rushed me over to my neighbor's house to tell her. She even made me raise my arms to show her! How embarrassing!"

"When I started growing pubic hair, it got annoying because **it was itchy!** Now it doesn't bother me so much anymore."

"I didn't know girls were supposed to have hair down there. It **freaked me out!**"

"The first time I noticed my body hair, I was afraid I would soon **become a werewolf!** Gah, I got so worried!"

"I was doing cartwheels in gymnastics when my teammate said, 'Hey, you have a little **dirt in your armpits.**' I looked, and it wasn't dirt—it was hair!"

3. You're getting hair everywhere.

You've always had hair on your arms and legs, but when you're a kid, that hair is usually light, soft, and hard to see. As you get older, that hair starts to grow darker and thicker, and you grow hair in your underarms, too. You also grow short, very curly hair called pubic hair around your private parts.

4. You're growing out and getting curvier.

With your body developing, you might start to notice that you're getting curvier. **Your hips and thighs will start getting wider,** which means clothes from the kids' section won't fit quite right anymore. This doesn't mean you're getting fat—**it's just a normal part of your body changing shape and looking more grown up.** Think of it as an opportunity for new clothes. Those cute jeans and dresses in the juniors' department are cut to fit your new figure!

> *When I started getting curves, I thought I was fat.*

You and your friends are probably developing at different paces. One girl may already have full hips while another girl's hips are still stick straight! **Everyone develops at different times into different shapes.** The size of your hips, your curves, your height, your shoe size—they're all pretty much decided by your genetics. Nobody will ever have your unique, amazing body or look just like you!

WHY are all these things happening?

Hormones, that's why! Hormones are chemicals that help your body function and grow. Different hormones have different jobs in your body. Your puberty hormones are called estrogen and testosterone. **In general, girls have a lot more estrogen and boys have a lot more testosterone—that's why girls' and boys' bodies develop differently.** So during puberty, when your breasts start growing, when you get your first period, and when you're feeling really emotional—that's thanks to estrogen!

> Estrogen: The hormone girls have more of that makes them develop curves and breasts, controls their period, and sometimes messes with their emotions.
>
> Testosterone: The hormone boys have more of that makes them grow facial hair and get deeper voices, and that sometimes messes with their emotions, too.

WHEN WILL IT HAPPEN to me? How do I know it's coming?

What makes puberty so confusing is that it starts at a different time for everybody. **Your best friend might start puberty when she's 8, and you might start when you're 13.** It doesn't mean that one of you is normal and one of you isn't—puberty just affects different bodies differently!

There's no way to know exactly when puberty will start for you, but we can give you some signs that it's coming...

Puberty is a little different for everyone!

Signs of Puberty

5'4

① Growth spurt.

5'0

4'8

4'4

4'0

② Nipples get **bigger** or puffier.

3'8

③ New hair
on underarms,
private parts,
and legs.

3'4

3'0

2'8

④ Hips and thighs
get wider.

2'4

2'0

⑤ Feet
get bigger
and stinkier.

⑥ Overall, you get a little **Sweatier** and a little *stinkier.*

66 Before I learned about puberty, I didn't know that so many other girls were plagued with the same issues as me. Now I can be more confident in knowing that I'm normal! 99

Puberty can be confusing, but it's also such an exciting time! **Imagine yourself as a caterpillar transforming into a beautiful butterfly.** And just like no two butterflies are exactly alike, you, too, are one of a kind. No one in the world will ever be just like you. You're changing from a girl into a strong, independent woman. **You're developing your own wings!**

Puberty isn't supposed to be scary. It can be pretty cool, too. Change can be hard, but it's always worth it when you start to fly!

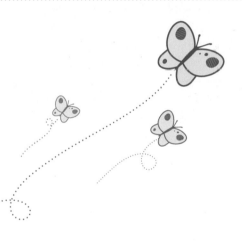

2

Breasts & Bras

The changes to my breasts did not surprise me, but my younger sister's friend had bigger breasts than me and this was shocking!

Your Breasts

One of the most noticeable changes that girls go through during puberty is that their breasts grow. Maybe yours have started growing already. Maybe you're still waiting (and waiting...and waiting!). **When it comes to breasts, every girl develops at her own pace** (just like all the other changes of puberty!), which can be totally frustrating.

If you're the first of your friends to develop, you might feel self-conscious. And if all your friends are wearing bras but you don't need one yet, that can make you feel weird, too. But don't forget that girls and women are all unique, and so are their breasts. **No matter when you develop breasts—or how large or small they are—they're just right for you.**

Of course, you probably have a lot of questions, like:

- When will my breasts grow?

- Does it hurt when they start growing?

- When will my breasts stop growing?

- How do I know my breasts are normal?

- How big will my breasts be?

- How can I make them grow faster (or slower)?

Well, try not to stress too much, because we're going to answer all your questions.

WHEN will my breasts grow and HOW BIG will they get?

Sometime between the ages of 8 and 16, your breasts will start to grow! Some girls start earlier and some later. You might feel like your breasts just grew overnight, and you can't figure out why you're so far ahead of your friends. Or you might feel like it's taking *forever* for them to grow, because all your friends have breasts already!

Your body decides when and how fast your breasts will grow—you can't speed them up or slow them down. You might start getting breasts later than your best friend, but end up with bigger breasts, or you might start developing early but end up with smaller breasts. **You can't predict how big they're going to be, either—but you can get a clue by looking at the other girls and women in your family.** If your mom started developing early, you're likely to also. If your mom and grandmothers have big breasts, you may get bigger breasts as well. If their breasts are small, yours are more likely to be small, too. But again, that's not always the case! As suspenseful as it is, you just have to wait and see.

HOW LONG will it take for my breasts to grow?

It'll take about three to five years for your breasts to grow, and they'll go through five stages of development. The first thing you'll notice is that the area underneath your nipples will start "budding," or sticking out a little. That little raised bump is called a "breast bud." Soon, your nipples and areolas (the darker skin surrounding the actual nipples) will grow bigger and darken a bit. Finally, your breasts will finish filling out and reach their adult size.

THE 5 STAGES OF BREAST DEVELOPMENT

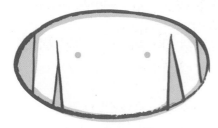

1 Before puberty, breasts haven't started to grow.

2 Breast buds start to develop.

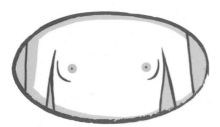

3 Breasts become rounder and bigger.

4 Nipples and areolas grow and stick out a little from the breasts.

5 Breasts fill out behind the nipples and stop growing.

What Girls Say...
Getting Breasts

"I was actually **excited about getting breasts.** I have always been a little behind my friends, so when I noticed my breasts were appearing, I was so happy!"

"I haven't started getting breasts yet. I'm worried that I might be the **last one in my group** of friends to develop."

"I thought I had something wrong with my breasts because they hurt and **one was bigger than the other,** but my mom told me this is normal."

"My breasts seemed too big for my body for a while, and I felt like everybody was **looking at me.**"

What will my breasts LOOK LIKE?

Breasts come in all different shapes and sizes. They can be big or small, round or pointed. Areolas look different on different girls, too. They can be lots of different colors, from pink to light brown to dark brown. It's common to have little bumps and hairs on your areolas, too. Even nipples vary. If yours face inward instead of pointing out, don't worry—plenty of girls have inverted nipples. Stay calm—it's all normal!

Will growing breasts HURT?

When they're growing, **your breasts might feel sore and hurt a little bit sometimes.** Lying on your stomach might be a

24

little uncomfortable, and it'll probably hurt more than it used to if something hits you in the chest. (When you score a goal in soccer, you might want to think twice before doing a victory chest bump with your bestie!) Most girls grow out of the soreness in a few weeks or months, but if you're really uncomfortable or it keeps getting worse, talk to your parents or your doctor.

What if one breast is BIGGER THAN THE OTHER?

Can everyone tell?

Your breasts might grow at different rates, and **one might be a little bigger than the other for a while—or forever!** Your smaller one might "catch up," but it's actually really common to have breasts that are slightly different in size. You probably never notice it on the women you know, and people won't notice it on you, either!

Sometimes it seems like every girl or woman would like to change something about her breasts. Girls with bigger breasts sometimes complain about having to wear a bra all the time. Girls with smaller breasts sometimes feel left out and wish their breasts were bigger. **But here's the thing about breasts: They're just as unique and special as the rest of you.** Instead of comparing yourself to someone else, **focus on embracing and loving the body you have!**

Bras

Now that we're talking breasts, we'd better talk about bras, too. **Yep, bras—one of the ultimate signs that you're becoming a woman!** In fact, you can even get a bra without having breasts. Maybe you've started to feel uncomfortable wearing just a shirt and want the extra coverage of a bra or cami. Or maybe you just want to wear a bra because everyone else is. For once, that's a perfectly acceptable reason!

Bras are really about making you feel comfortable in your own body, which can be pretty hard when it's changing so quickly.

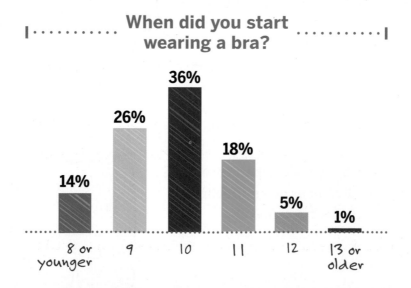

When did you start wearing a bra?

- 8 or younger: 14%
- 9: 26%
- 10: 36%
- 11: 18%
- 12: 5%
- 13 or older: 1%

1. They protect and support!

Bras help support your breasts so they feel comfortable and secure, especially when you're playing sports!

2. They make you feel less exposed!

A bra covers up your breasts and nipples if you're wearing a light-colored or tight shirt, so you don't have to worry that someone can see more than you'd like!

3. They can add a nice shape!

A bra helps shape your breasts into a silhouette that looks nice under your clothes.

· · · · · · · · · · · · · · · · · · 🦋 ·

HOW DO I KNOW I need a bra?

Many girls choose to start wearing a bra or cami before their breasts have really developed (and that's fine!), but some prefer to wait until they really need one. If you're not sure whether you need a bra yet, ask yourself these questions:

- *Can I see my nipples through my shirt?*
- *Is my chest sore or uncomfortable when I run or play sports?*
- *Do I feel self-conscious about my chest sometimes?*
- *Will a bra make me feel more comfortable and self-confident?*
- *Will a bra make my clothes fit or feel better?*

If you answered yes to any of these, it's probably time for a bra!

DID YOU KNOW?

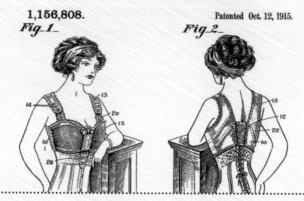

1,156,808.
Fig. 1

Patented Oct. 12, 1915.
Fig. 2

Modern bras first became popular in the 1920s. Small breasts were in style, so the bra was designed to flatten rather than support them.

If you do want to start wearing a bra, it might seem embarrassing to ask for one, but you can handle it! Both your parents—yes, even your dad—know what it's like to go through changes during puberty. Once you get the asking part over with, you'll wonder why you ever worried about it at all. Just think of how fun it will be to have an exciting new shopping experience! When in doubt, keep it simple. "I think I'd be more comfortable wearing a bra. Can we go shopping?" If it's still too embarrassing to say out loud, try writing a note. (Just don't leave it where your brother might find it first!)

TIP

If you don't want to wear a bra yet, but your parents say it's time, listen to them! They're looking out for you—and probably trying to save you from embarrassment.

"I liked how it felt. I felt like I could fit in better and *I loved wearing one.*"

"*I was scared to ask,* but one night I just dove in. My mom looked surprised, but I think she remembered what it was like when she was my age and said, 'Sure.' I was so happy that I had gotten over it."

"I felt okay about getting a bra because I needed one, and when the time is right, you just need to face the fact and *step out of your comfort zone.*"

"I wanted to get a bra to *feel more grown up* and developed. I think bras are more comfortable than no bras."

"The first bra I tried on was *itchy and tight!* How was I supposed to wear it every day? Then, I tried on another one, and it was more comfortable."

"*I felt cool getting my first bra!* I always wore an undershirt, so it wasn't too different."

"I didn't want to get a bra. *I was annoyed* because I thought it was stupid that girls have to do that."

How do I know WHAT SIZE BRA to get?

A bra size has two parts—a number and a letter. (For example, 32A.) The number represents how big the bra is around your chest and back (your band size), while the letter represents how big your actual breast is (your cup size).

Band Size   **32A**   Cup Size

Bra sizing is confusing, so you'll probably want help finding your size from your mom or the saleswoman in a lingerie department. (Lingerie saleswomen are specially trained and can be a huge help!) You'll also want to try on a bunch of bras, since even if a bra is labeled with your size, it may not look or feel right on you. **The only way to know if it fits is to try it on.** (When trying on bras with three rows of hooks in the back, always judge the fit using the middle hooks.) **Find out how to measure your bra size on the next page!**

Find out how to measure your bra size on the next page!

TIP

You can wear a bra three to four times before washing it, unless you sweat a lot. Wash your bras by hand or on a washing machine's "delicate" cycle, and then let them air dry.

HOW TO
MEASURE YOUR BRA SIZE

STEP 1: Find Your Band Size

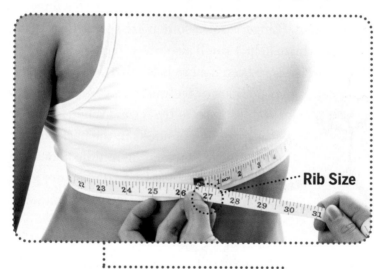

Rib Size

With a tape measure, measure **around your ribs directly below your breasts.** If the measurement is an even number, add 4. If it's odd, add 5. The total is the size of your band.

Example:

27	+	5	=	32
(Odd Rib Size)				(Band Size)

28	+	4	=	32
(Even Rib Size)				(Band Size)

STEP 2: Find Your Cup Size

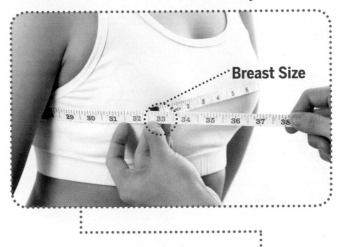

Breast Size

For your cup size, measure **around your body at the level of the fullest part of your chest.** Subtract your band size from this number. This will be the size, or letter, of your cup.

Example:

33	–	32	=	1
(Breast Size)		(Band Size)		(Cup Number)

Find your cup letter:

Cup Number	-1	0	1	2	3	4
Cup Letter	AAA	AA	A	B	C	D

STEP 3: Find Your Bra Size

Put your band size and cup size together to get your bra size!

Example:

32	A
(Band)	(Cup)

There are four basic bra styles—check out the following pages to help you decide which one you like best!

The Cami

Camis are a great way to ease into wearing a bra if you're not ready for a real one, but still want something to wear under a top. Some even have built-in bra linings!

I wear camis with built-in bras every day just because I like the extra support. It's more comfortable just to have a cami on every day.

The Training Bra

Most girls' first bras are training bras. No, they don't train your breasts to grow! They train *you* to get used to wearing bras! They are stretchy and comfy and feel sort of like wearing half a cami.

“ *I felt self-conscious because other girls were wearing bras when I wasn't. Training bras are a great first step—I feel more confident, and it helps me get used to the feeling of wearing a bra.* ”

TIP
If you sweat a lot in your sports bras, wash them after each time you wear them!

These bras are made to give you lots of support when you're playing sports, but you can wear them any time you want. Some girls find the support and wider straps on sports bras more comfortable and secure.

> *I'm very active and to me, sports bras are the most comfortable. They feel just like a cut off tank top, and they are similar to dance rehearsal clothes or bathing suits.*

If you're more developed, you might want to try a fashion bra. The hooks in the back are a bit tricky, but you can also get bras that close in front. They usually have plastic or wire built into the lining for extra support, so sometimes they're called underwire bras.

My personal favorite is an underwire bra, because it gives a lot of support. The wire feels a little uncomfortable at first, but you get used to it quickly!

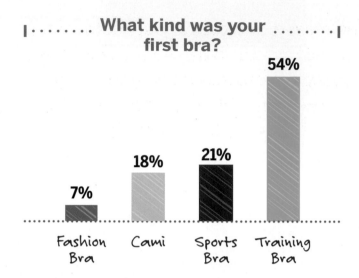

What kind was your first bra?

- 7% — Fashion Bra
- 18% — Cami
- 21% — Sports Bra
- 54% — Training Bra

Bras are undergarments—not outerwear for people to see!—so you don't want yours to show through your clothes. Check out this chart to help you decide which bra to wear with your clothes.

BRA COLOR	TOP OR DRESS COLOR
Flesh Tone Colors	Wear under any color!
White	Wear under colors only—don't wear under white!
Black	Wear under black or navy.
Bright Colors	Wear under black, navy, or bright colors.
Patterned or Multi-colored	Wear under black, navy, or bright colors.

Getting breasts and bras is just another step toward becoming a young woman. Since you can't speed the process up or stop it from happening, you might as well relax and enjoy it. Soon, you'll be ready to go shopping...**there's a whole new world of cute bras out there, just waiting for you!**

When you get your first bra, it may seem weird. When I got mine, I was a little embarrassed. But now it feels weird without one!

3

Your Period

All About Your Period

"Aunt Flo," your "monthly visitor," "that time of the month" (or TOM). For generations, girls and women have had special names for their periods, and you and your friends probably will, too. Whatever you call it, **getting your period is the most important change your body will go through during puberty.** It's amazing when you think about it—it's as if **you share a special bond with girls and women all around the world, in every culture!**

Even though it's exciting that you're becoming a woman, there *are* things about getting your period that are annoying. It's never easy to be the first or the last of your friends to start, and cramps and moodiness are no fun, either. But guess what? Understanding and mastering your period can actually make you feel empowered! And that's what we're going to help you do now!

DID YOU KNOW?

In Native American cultures, a girl's first period is celebrated with feasts that last for days, ritual dancing and chanting, and gifts. Many tribes also consider women having their period to be very powerful spiritually.

Every girl before you has gone through it and survived—so can you!

54% of girls find **periods the most stressful part** of puberty.

Wrong Ideas About Periods

"I thought it would be noticeable, but it's not. **No one even knows** I've started, except my mom."

"I thought you **only got it once,** not every month."

"I thought it came out my **pee** hole."

"I thought I'd never be able to **go swimming again!**"

"I thought tons of blood would come out, **like a hose!**"

"I thought it would be just a little blood and it would stay **every day of my life!**"

"I thought I would be able to **feel it coming out,** but I can't."

Before you can understand your period, you need to know what's *down there*. So let's get the awkward stuff over with first, as simply as possible.

This is what your girly parts look like from outside your body. Grab a mirror and take a look...seriously! Maybe that sounds like a weird thing to do, but this is your body, and no one should know it better than you. **So push past the embarrassment, lock the bathroom door, and take a good look.** You'll feel more confident if you know your body better.

⊦·········· You on the Outside ·········⊦

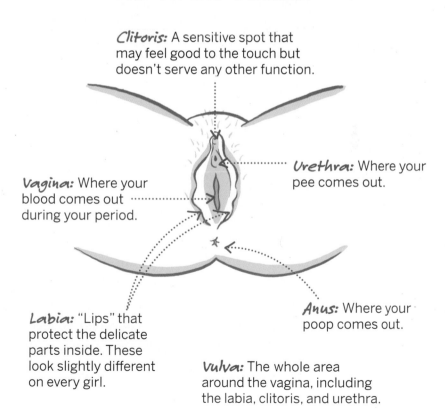

Clitoris: A sensitive spot that may feel good to the touch but doesn't serve any other function.

Urethra: Where your pee comes out.

Vagina: Where your blood comes out during your period.

Anus: Where your poop comes out.

Labia: "Lips" that protect the delicate parts inside. These look slightly different on every girl.

Vulva: The whole area around the vagina, including the labia, clitoris, and urethra.

Now let's take a look at the inside. This part is more important when we're talking about where your period comes from.

You on the Inside

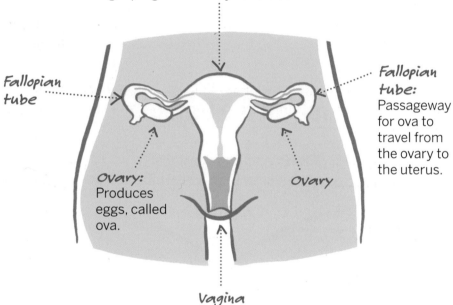

Uterus: Where a baby will grow if you get pregnant when you're older.

Fallopian tube

Fallopian tube: Passageway for ova to travel from the ovary to the uterus.

Ovary: Produces eggs, called ova.

Ovary

Vagina

During puberty, your body starts getting ready for the possibility of being pregnant, even though you won't be worrying about that for a long time. Every month, your uterus builds up a lining of blood and nutrients. Someday, if you do decide to have a baby, the lining will protect and take care of the baby as it grows inside you. But as long as there is no baby, the lining isn't needed, so it comes out every month through your vagina—and that's your period!

When will I get MY FIRST PERIOD?

Most girls start their periods between ages 10 and 12, but you might start anywhere between ages 8 and 15—it's all normal and healthy! Periods happen when your body is ready, and every girl is on her own schedule. If you're worried, ask your mom or older sister how old she was when she started hers. You'll probably start around the same age as your female family members.

Even though we can't tell you exactly when you'll have your first period, there are some signs to watch for. A few months before your first period, you might have some vaginal discharge—a clear or white fluid about the thickness of mucus—in your underwear. That's one of the first signs that your body is getting ready for your first period.

For a few days right before your period, you might be a little uncomfortable—many girls get headaches, stomachaches, sore breasts, or cramps in their lower belly. You might also see a few drops of blood in your underwear.

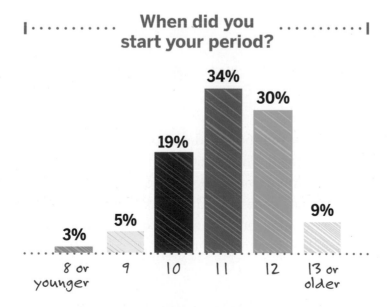

When did you start your period?

3% — 8 or younger
5% — 9
19% — 10
34% — 11
30% — 12
9% — 13 or older

What will my period FEEL LIKE?

Some girls say having their period feels like needing to pee. Even though your period doesn't come out of the same place your pee does, it might still feel similar. Some girls feel wetness in their underwear, and other girls don't feel anything at all and only realize that they've started their period when they see blood in their underwear!

HOW MUCH WILL I BLEED and what will it LOOK LIKE?

Most—but not *all*—girls only bleed for three to five days, and only bleed heavily for a couple of those days. On the first day of your period, the blood might be:

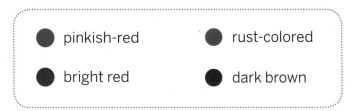

- pinkish-red
- bright red
- rust-colored
- dark brown

Toward the end of your period, the blood may be a darker brown and have a sour smell. That's totally normal—it just means that it's been in your uterus longer. Sounds icky, right? Well, trust every woman who's gone through it before—it might be a bit gross in the beginning, but it's nothing to worry about. As time goes by, it will feel more natural to you!

My First Period

"I was using the restroom and *bam*! I realized my period was actually here. I didn't have any pads so I **folded up a bunch of toilet paper.** I did this for the next two months until I worked up the courage to tell my mom."

"I had cramps and had to **use the bathroom a lot** for two days. It was weird, but one day at home I had blood. It wasn't a big problem."

"Honestly, **I had nightmares** about starting my period in public. I was afraid I would be **embarrassed for life!** But when I first saw this weird brownish-red stuff on my underwear, I was like, 'Where did this come from? I never noticed it before.'"

"I freaked out when I saw the blood and **started yelling for my mom.** She calmed me down and explained what happened."

"When I first got it, **I thought I pooped** myself (it was brown). But when I put my pants in the laundry, my mom said I had started my period."

HOW OFTEN will I get my period?

A period is called that because it happens periodically—approximately once a month. At first, your period might not follow a regular schedule. It can come every other month, twice a month, or be just plain unpredictable! You might even skip a period or two. It may be annoying, but all you can do is wait it out. Within a couple of years, your body should develop a predictable schedule—your period should come about every 28 days, though everyone's cycle is a little different. Yours might be anywhere from 21 to 45 days and still be perfectly normal.

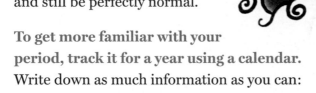

To get more familiar with your period, track it for a year using a calendar. Write down as much information as you can:

- How heavy was your flow each day?

- Did you have **cramps** or **headaches**?

- Did you feel **moody** or **irritable** right before or during your period?

These notes will help you predict when your period will come the next time. You'll know which days you should wear a panty liner or light pad "just in case" and be able to avoid those embarrassing "I-have-to-run-to-the-bathroom-right-now!" moments.

TIP
Create your own secret code to keep track of your period!
✳ + X ✓

• Light Flow •• Medium Flow •ᣞ Heavy Flow

⊗ Feel cramps or headaches

☹ Feel moody or irritable

Menstrual Cycle: If you count the days from the first day of one period to the first day of your next period, that's one "menstrual cycle." "Menstruation" is just a fancy word for your period, so your menstrual cycle is from one period to the next.

Pads & Tampons

Once you have your period, **it can feel like a secret world of products** has just opened up to you! That aisle in the drug or grocery store is no longer off limits, but what do you make of all the options? There isn't just one type of pad, there are a gazillion! And all the tampon types can be even more confusing! Don't worry—**we'll break it down so you know what that aisle is all about.**

DID YOU KNOW?

SEARS CATALOG, 1908

Before pads were invented, women wore towels with belts attached to them! At least you don't have to deal with that! Thank goodness for modern technology!

What are PADS?

Pads are the simplest of panty protectors. **A pad is just a cotton-like material that sticks to your underwear and soaks up the blood.** They come in different sizes—thinner ones for days when you're bleeding less, and thicker ones for when you're bleeding more. Some pads even have wings that wrap around your panty and keep the pad from moving around. Pads are also sometimes called maxi pads, sanitary pads, or sanitary napkins.

During the day, **you should check your pad every three to four hours** to see if it needs to be changed. If you wait for four hours or more, you might notice an unpleasant smell. That doesn't mean you need to use scented pads, which can irritate your sensitive skin! It just means you should change your pad more often and practice good hygiene (more on that later!).

Most girls like to start out with pads for their first periods, and many girls and women use only pads. But there's one time you definitely should not wear a pad—when you're swimming! They'll soak up lots of water and feel super bulky. And the sticky strips might lose their stick—you don't want the pad coming off in the water!

You'll probably also **need some panty liners.** They're small, extra-thin pads that are perfect for days when you have barely any bleeding, or "flow." Panty liners are also handy when you're expecting your period but don't know exactly when it will come, or for a little extra protection when you're wearing a tampon.

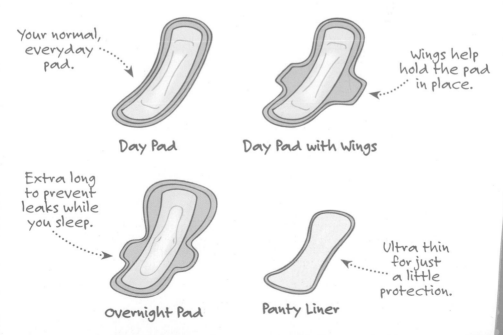

Your normal, everyday pad.

Day Pad

Wings help hold the pad in place.

Day Pad with Wings

Extra long to prevent leaks while you sleep.

Overnight Pad

Ultra thin for just a little protection.

Panty Liner

What are TAMPONS?

Tampons are more confusing. A tampon is a bit of **cotton-like material that you insert into your vagina** to soak up the blood. Think of it as a tiny pad that goes *inside* you instead of being attached to your underwear. Some girls love tampons because you can't feel them once they're in. They're also great for swimming, when you really *can't* wear a pad, and for sports like gymnastics or dance, when the outline of a pad might show under a leotard.

Just like pads, **tampons come in several sizes.** You can also get them with or without an applicator, which is just a little plastic covering that helps you put the tampon in.

Here's what a tampon with an applicator looks like:

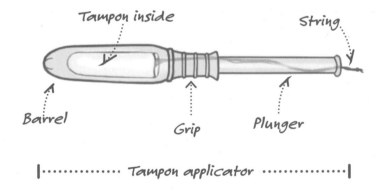

Tampon inside

String

Barrel

Grip

Plunger

|·············· Tampon applicator ···············|

The downside to a tampon is that **it's harder to use than a pad.** There are instructions in every box of tampons, but don't worry—we'll show you how to use them, too!

WRONG IDEAS
about TAMPONS
Corrected!

It hurts to have a tampon in!
No! Once it's in, you can't feel a tampon. At all.

**That whole big plastic applicator
goes up inside you.**
Only a small part of the plastic applicator goes
inside you, and only long enough for you to push the
tampon into place. Then you take the applicator out
and throw it away.

The tampon might fall right out again!
As a tampon absorbs your period blood, it expands
a little to fit the shape of your vagina. It can't fall out.

A tampon can get stuck inside you!
All it takes is a gentle tug on the string and the
tampon slides right out. And the string can't
come off—it's woven into the tampon itself, so
no worries there!

The tampon can travel up inside you and get lost!
There's nowhere for the tampon to go. It will
stay in place until you decide to pull it out.

How to Use a Tampon

1 Unwrap the tampon and hold the applicator at the grip. Then gently push the barrel into your vagina.

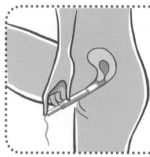

2 When the barrel is all the way in, press the plunger with your index finger to push the tampon into place.

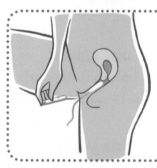

3 Once the tampon is in place, pull out the applicator (but leave the string!) and throw it away.

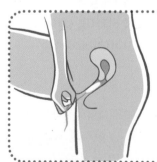

4 After 3 to 6 hours, gently pull on the string, and *voilà*—it's out!

TIP

It's easier to put in a tampon if you squat slightly or stand with one foot up on the toilet seat.

HOW LONG are you supposed to leave the tampon in?

Listen up! This is very important: **Do not leave your tampon in for more than six hours.** Wearing a tampon for too long increases the risk of Toxic Shock Syndrome (TSS), a very rare but very bad disease. (See the next page for more information.) You'll usually need to **change your tampon every three to six hours.** You can change it more often, but if you take it out when it's still dry, it might hurt a little. As you become more familiar with your cycle, you'll know how often to change it.

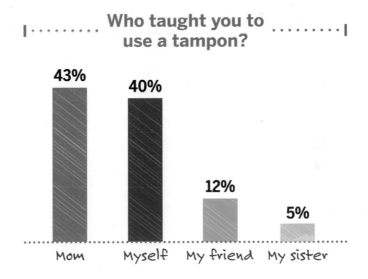

I . . . . **Who taught you to use a tampon?** I

43% Mom
40% Myself
12% My friend
5% My sister

IMPORTANT: Tampons should only be used when you have your period—not for the normal discharge you get when you're not on your period. The purpose of that discharge is to flush out bad bacteria. That can't be done if it stays inside you!

Toxic Shock Syndrome

Toxic Shock Syndrome (TSS) is an **extremely rare but serious disease** that can be caused by wearing a tampon too long. Because tampons absorb your period blood inside your body, it's possible for bacteria to grow there, and those bacteria can become toxic to your body. We know all this sounds scary, but **tampons are designed to be safe,** and there is very little chance that you'll get TSS from wearing one. Still, it's important to follow these guidelines to be as safe as possible.

- *Never* leave a tampon in for more than six hours and never wear one overnight.

- Use more absorbent tampons only when your flow is heavy. Use less absorbent tampons or pads on lighter days.

If you're using tampons and you start to develop any of these symptoms, **immediately** take out your tampon and tell an adult.

- Fever of 102 degrees or higher.

- Dizziness, fainting, headaches, confusion, or seizure.

- Sunburn-like rash, vomiting, diarrhea, or severe muscle aches.

TIP

Pad, tampon, or panty liner...whatever you're using, it's super important to wash your hands both before and after changing it.

Tampons vs. Pads

"I think that having something up my 'parts' just **seems uncomfortable and scary.** Sometimes I think I am the only girl who uses pads, but I'm good with them for now."

"I only use pads. I can't really tell when tampons are full like a pad, and **I'm scared of leaking!**"

"I was always afraid of inserting a tampon, and thought it would hurt. I have learned, however, that it **doesn't even feel like it's there!** Now I love them!"

"I used a tampon for the first time when I really **wanted to go swimming.** I love swimming, and now tampons are part of my bag of period supplies."

How do I THROW AWAY my USED PADS and TAMPONS?

The number one rule: **throw it in the trash, not the toilet!** Some tampons say "flushable" on the box, but the plumbing in some houses still can't handle them. So play it safe and put it in the trash. Just wrap it up in some toilet paper or the wrapper of your new pad or tampon, and toss it—that's all! That way, you **won't** have to **deal with** the embarrassment of a **clogged toilet** on top of everything else.

Being Prepared

Sometimes having your period can feel like one big surprise! When will it come? Will you be ready? If you're stressed that your period will catch you off guard, **take control** and **be prepared.** Keep an **"emergency period kit"** in your backpack or locker at all times. Throw in a couple of pads or tampons and a clean pair of undies. **You'll feel much more calm if you're in control!**

What if my first period SURPRISES ME?

If your period totally sneaks up on you, **don't panic!** Most public bathrooms have a vending machine with pads. **If you're really stuck, fold up a few layers of toilet paper** and place them in your underwear. Then ask a mom, a teacher, a school nurse, a friend who's already gotten her period, or any other female you trust if she has an extra pad. Announcing your first period to someone may seem like the last thing you want to do, but remember, she had to go through *her* first period, too. She'll understand!

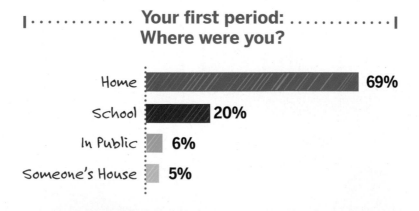

Your first period: Where were you?

Home	69%
School	20%
In Public	6%
Someone's House	5%

DID YOU KNOW?

69% of girls get **cramps.**

58% of girls feel **moody or sensitive.**

51% of girls get **breast tenderness.**

Will my period HURT?

As if the blood weren't enough to handle, periods bring cramps, too. **Cramps are pains in your tummy area** that come around the time of your period. (Some girls also feel pain in their lower back or upper thighs during their period. Some also experience sore breasts right before or during their period.) The muscles of your uterus have to squeeze in order to push out the lining, and all that squeezing causes cramps. **Cramps are perfectly normal,** but they can feel pretty uncomfortable! The good news is **there's a lot you can do to relieve the pain.**

TIP

If you have a locker, keep a spare pair of jeans or pants inside at all times. They may come in handy if you leak blood onto your clothes. Even a sweater to tie around your waist can help!

Helpful Tips
⊢··· BEST WAYS TO RELIEVE CRAMPS ···⊣

Don't let cramps get the best of you—try these tricks!

1. Exercise

Running around the block may not sound like much
fun when your insides are hurting, but getting your
blood flowing is the best thing you can do. Exercise loosens up
your muscles and boosts your mood. If you can't bring yourself to
go for a run, try something gentler, like stretching or yoga.

2. Hydration

Before your period, your body tends to hold onto extra water,
which can make you feel bloated and worsen your cramps. It
sounds odd, but if you drink lots of water, your body flushes
out the extra fluid...and you feel better!

3. Medicine

You'll have to ask your mom or dad about this one, but if they say it's
okay, an anti-inflammatory like ibuprofen can really help.

4. Heat

A heating pad or a warm bath helps relax your
muscles, and relaxed muscles mean fewer cramps.
Warm drinks help, too!

Hopefully your cramps aren't too bad—some girls don't get them at
all! However, if they're so bad that they're interfering with your daily
activities, you should talk to a doctor to see if there are better ways to
relieve them.

Exercise can help your cramps, especially when it's something that you enjoy doing. Playing a sport helps ease my cramps and takes my mind off it.

Helpful Tips
ON LEAKS AND STAINS

Leaking blood onto your pants (or your sheets while you sleep) is very common. Don't worry—here's help!

1. Wash It Out

Rinse or soak the stain in cold water and a little detergent or stain remover. Don't use hot water—it will make the stain permanent.

2. Be Prepared

Prevent stains by wearing a panty liner if you think your period is coming soon.

3. Dress Wisely

Avoid wearing light-colored pants or skirts during your period, just in case!

4. Sleep Safe

At night, wear pads that are extra-long and made for overnight protection. You can also sleep with a towel under your hips to protect your sheets.

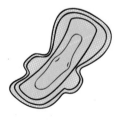

Knowing about all the changes your body will go through when you start you period, **you'll feel more prepared, confident, and empowered.**

> *It's okay if you get your period at 10 years old or if you get it at 14 years old. It doesn't make you crazy or weird to change at a different time than all your friends. Periods and puberty are just a part of life—every girl has to go through them. Remember, other girls around the world are dealing with the same issues as you. You are not alone!*

4

Your Emotions

Your Emotions

Your mom looks at you the wrong way and you scream your head off. Your crush says hi to you and you're smiling all day. You step on an ant and cry your eyes out for hours. **Welcome to the emotional roller coaster that is puberty!**

Even if you're normally the most easygoing person, you can expect your new hormones to change that, at least a little. All those **hormones can intensify your emotions,** making something sad feel like an all-out tragedy—or something happy feel like the best thing that ever happened to you. And **while hormones can't control you completely,** it can certainly feel like they're **messing with your head** a bit.

> *I feel more emotional during certain times of the month. I even cried once when a meatball rolled off my plate onto the floor. I get annoyed with my hair and find little things ridiculous, and then, bam, the following day, everything goes back to normal. It's like there are two of me: the exaggerated version and the 'go with the flow' version.*

There's nothing you can do to stop these feelings from coming, so your best defense is to know that you're *not* crazy and learn to deal with them. If you keep track of your moods and periods on a calendar, **you may start to notice a pattern.** Maybe you always get emotional or have a headache right before your period starts. Paying more attention to your moods can help you predict when you're more likely to be upset. You may even want to try to **avoid emotionally charged situations on those days.**

June

Su	Mo	Tu	We	Th	Fr	Sa
1	2	3	4	5	6	7
8	9	10	11	12	13	14
15	16	17	18	19	20	21
22	23	24	25	26	27	28
29	30					

- • Light Flow
- •• Medium Flow
- ••• Heavy Flow
- ☹ Feel moody or irritable
- ⊗ Feel cramps or headaches

> *I used to blame getting upset easily on lack of sleep, but then I noticed that every time it happened, I'd start my period. After that I realized that they were related.*

"Sixth grade was the worst year for me for hormones and mood swings. *I cried almost every night!* I still have trouble handling my emotions, but I'm getting better."

"Right before I get my period, I feel tired, grouchy, and like I want to *bite everybody's head off.*"

"I get *angry at my friends,* who normally never make me mad."

"I feel very tired and *get upset very easily* over things that are not a big deal. Even stupid things, like what I should eat for an after-school snack."

"One day, I watched a movie that was really sad, but I didn't react to it. The next day, I watched it again and I cried my eyes out the whole time! *Nothing had changed*—it was just my hormones!"

"Sometimes I feel like *throwing things* out the window!"

"I get really moody and *cry for no reason.* Then I cry because I'm upset that I'm crying for no reason! It's really irritating!"

Hormones or Real Emotions?

When you have so many ups and downs, it's easy to get confused about what's going on with your feelings. Your body is changing so fast you barely recognize it, you're taking on more responsibilities at home and at school, and you've got all that social pressure, too (cliques, drama, mean girls... need we say more?).

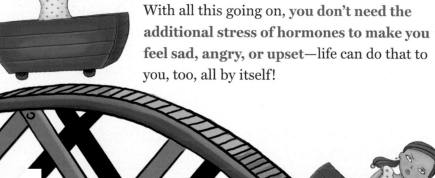

With all this going on, **you don't need the additional stress of hormones to make you feel sad, angry, or upset**—life can do that to you, too, all by itself!

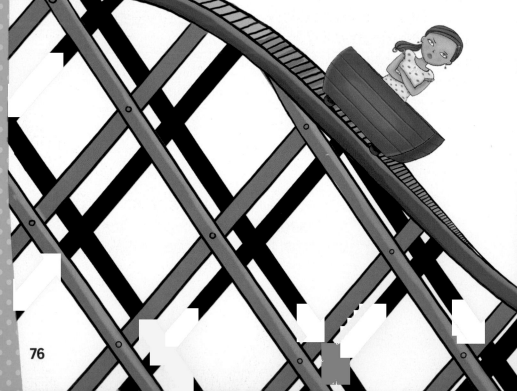

So how can you tell if your emotions are normal reactions or if your hormones are messing with you? Just ask yourself these questions:

What happened today?
What changed since yesterday?

Let's try it out. Say you were your normal, cheerful self yesterday. You had a great time hanging out with your friends, and when you looked in the mirror, you noticed how shiny your hair was and how pretty your eyes looked. Then today you woke up, looked in the mirror, and thought, "I'm so ugly. Everybody hates me."

What now? Ask yourself what happened. What changed since yesterday? The answer, of course, is nothing. You still have the same shiny hair and pretty eyes you had then. Your friends haven't all turned against you overnight. The only thing that has changed is what's going on in your head...and that's how you know your hormones are probably messing with your emotions.

Of course, **not all your negative emotions come from your hormones.** If you just found out your best friend is moving away or your grandma is seriously ill, you've got a very real reason to be upset. But no matter where your feelings are coming from, **it's your responsibility to deal with them**—you don't get to take your bad mood out on other people! Don't worry...that's something we can definitely help you with!

Managing Your Emotions

Often, the best way to change your mood is to change your thinking. Did you know that your emotions are a direct result of your thoughts? Your thoughts come first, and your emotions follow along. **When you think negative thoughts, you feel negative emotions.**

Let's look at an example to see how that works.

You just missed a goal in soccer and cost your team the game. You're disappointed, sad, and embarrassed that you let your team down. Here are two possible ways you might think about the loss:

Negative:

"I can't believe I missed that goal. I'm such a loser. Obviously, I suck at soccer. They'll probably kick me off the team tomorrow, and I don't blame them."

Positive:

"I'm so upset I missed that goal. I had a bad day today, but I know I did my best. I'll keep practicing, and I'll do better next time."

Your situation is the same either way—you can't change what happened. But with **negative** thinking, you're **hurting your self-esteem.** You're just stuck feeling bad about yourself. With the more positive thoughts, your self-esteem isn't hurt and you feel you can do better next time. You're still disappointed about what happened, but you're giving yourself the encouragement you need to keep going—and ultimately, to keep getting better.

"Nobody likes me. I feel so alone."

"It's like a party in my head!"

7 Great Ways to Manage Your Mood

1. Move Your Body

We can't say enough good things about exercise! Have you ever noticed how you feel happier and have a sense of accomplishment after a good workout? That's because **working out creates endorphins— body chemicals that make us feel happy.** No matter how low you're feeling, your mood will get a well-deserved boost after a workout. Exercise also helps keep your heart in shape, makes you stronger and more flexible, builds your endurance, and helps you stay at a healthy weight. And exercise is totally fun—and it's great for your self-esteem, too!

Nothing changes my state of mind like running. I can be having the worst day ever, but after a good run, it just doesn't seem so bad anymore.

2. Talk About It

Don't hold in all those feelings until you're ready to explode! Friends can be a great source of support, since you're all in the same boat. (Just be sure you only share your feelings with friends you're absolutely sure you can trust—the last thing you need is to have your troubles blabbed to the entire school!) And don't forget your mom—she went through puberty once, too, and may understand more than you realize. Even talking to your pet can help—**just saying things out loud can help you see things differently and calm you down.**

> *Having someone you can share everything with (yes, even your period and moodiness) is so-o-o important! It's how I get through my days sometimes!*

3. Laugh—a Lot!

Humor can rescue you from a mortifying moment or make you feel better when you're in a foul mood. No matter what's going on, **the ability to laugh at yourself and your situation is really important.** And did you know that just **smiling can help** to put you in a better mood? It's true! Using your smile muscles tells your brain to make more endorphins, and that boosts your mood!

> *Whenever I'm in a bad mood, my friend does something silly to crack me up. I start laughing so much, I forget what I was upset about in the first place!*

4. Say You're Sorry

I'm SORRY!!

No matter how good you are at managing your emotions, you'll still occasionally slip up and say something you regret. (You're only human!) **Just take a deep breath and apologize.** You'll feel better if you do!

> *When my emotions take over, I just apologize if I've made a mean comment. The people who care about you most, like your family and friends, are the best people around—they'll understand!*

5. Recharge

To calm your mind, **calm your body!** Soaking away the sad feelings in a warm bubble bath, listening to soothing music, or reading a good book can help you quiet your thoughts and **get a better perspective** on whatever is bugging you.

> *When I'm feeling moody, I like to pamper myself with a hot bubble bath and then do my nails. It helps to have some time to just clear my mind.*

6. Cry—It's Okay!

Sometimes the only way to get your feelings out is to cry— so go ahead! Shut yourself in your room and bawl your eyes out! **No one says you have to be happy all the time.** When you're done, you'll be ready to face the world again.

> *If I'm sad, I cry with my stuffed animals, and then I feel better.*

7. Get Creative

Draw, write, paint, sing, dance, play music...! Do something that makes you feel like you're **getting all your emotions out in a creative way**—it feels awesome!

> *I like to write down how I feel. It helps me catch up on my thoughts and everything that goes on (like friend drama). It puts everything in a better perspective.*

11% of tweens and teens **suffer from depression.***

If you have depression, you feel sad all the time for two weeks or longer, and you have two or more of the following feelings.**

- *You don't want to spend time with your friends or family.*

- *You've lost interest in activities you used to love.*

- *You can't get out of bed—every morning.*

- *You think you're not good enough and that no one cares about you.*

- *You want to run away from home, hurt yourself, or hurt someone else.*

- *You feel hopeless, like nothing will ever get better.*

If this sounds like you, talk to your mom, dad, teacher, or another adult you trust right away. **Please don't be afraid to reach out.** If the first person doesn't help you, tell someone else. **The sooner you get help, the sooner you can start feeling happy again.**

*Source: National Institute of Mental Health (nimh.nih.org)
**Source: American Academy of Child and Adolescent Psychiatry (aacap.org)

"After my doctor put me on a new medication, *my depression slowly started melting away.* I started hanging out with my friends again, and I realized how much I'd missed them. My teachers noticed that I was my outgoing, bubbly self again. They liked it, and so did I!"

"If you think you have depression, please talk to your parents or an adult you trust. They can get you the help you need. Just *remember that you are not alone.* Talk to someone and your life may just completely turn around. Mine did."

"Slowly but surely, with the *help of my doctor and my family and friends,* my depression got better. During this journey, I realized how strong I really am mentally. I got back to being the independent, upbeat, happy girl that I used to be, and it feels great!"

IMPORTANT: The official definition of depression says it's a feeling of sadness that lasts for two weeks or more, but you don't have to wait for two weeks to ask for help. **Any time you feel overwhelmed by sadness, worry, or hopelessness, talk to an adult you trust.** Just like these girls who got help, you deserve to feel better!

The emotional changes you'll go through can be **one of the most difficult parts of puberty,** but we can tell you that you're definitely not alone. Even people who seem to have it all together have struggled with the same feelings you're having. The tools we've given you in this chapter will help you **get through even your toughest moments.**

> *Puberty is an emotional roller coaster! But it's easier when you understand your emotions, because you learn that there's actually a reason why you just randomly feel grouchy. When you understand it, you can better control yourself!*

5

Skin Care
& Acne

Quiz

WHAT'S YOUR SKIN TYPE?

1. **In the morning, my skin usually feels:**

a. Like the Sahara Desert...so dry!

b. Pretty normal. I can go without washing my face or putting moisturizer on it.

c. Oily and slick. My face is shinier than a freshly waxed car!

d. Normal or dry in some parts and oily in others.

2. **My face tends to break out:**

a. Hardly ever! And when it does, it's still flaky and dry!

b. Now and then...usually just around my period.

c. All the time and all over—no matter how much I scrub and scrub.

d. On certain parts, like my forehead, chin, and nose. But not usually on my cheeks.

3. **By mid-afternoon, my face is:**

a. Itchy and flaky and driving me nuts.

b. Same old, same old. Can't complain...

c. Already back to shiny and slick!

d. Acting like it has a split personality: parts of it are oily, but other parts aren't.

WHAT'S YOUR SKIN TYPE?

············· If you answered... ·············

Mostly A's: You probably* have DRY SKIN.

But just because your skin is dry doesn't mean you can skip washing your face! Your pores can still get clogged with sweat and dead skin cells. Wash twice a day with a facial cleanser for dry skin—once in the morning and once at night—and **apply a hydrating moisturizer** after each time. You may also want to apply moisturizer to dry spots throughout the day. And stay away from toners and astringents—they'll dry your skin out even more.

Mostly B's: You probably* have NORMAL SKIN.

Lucky you! Your skin is not too dry and not too oily. You're not free and clear, though! You still need to keep your face clean. (Nobody gets out of that!) **Wash your face twice a day with a gentle cleanser** to maintain your great skin. And if a pimple does strike, spot-treat it with a bit of salicylic acid–based zit cream.

*What's with the asterisks next to the word "probably" in each answer?

Your skin's type isn't set in stone—it's going through a process. Your skin texture may change from year to year or even month to month!

Mostly C's: You probably* have OILY SKIN.

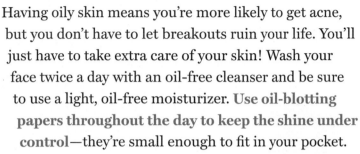

Having oily skin means you're more likely to get acne, but you don't have to let breakouts ruin your life. You'll just have to take extra care of your skin! Wash your face twice a day with an oil-free cleanser and be sure to use a light, oil-free moisturizer. **Use oil-blotting papers throughout the day to keep the shine under control**—they're small enough to fit in your pocket. Try applying toner or astringent with a cotton pad every other night. If it dries out your skin too much, it's not for you, but if it seems to help, you can try increasing your use to every day. Spot-treat pimples with a benzoyl peroxide–based cream.

Mostly D's: You probably* have COMBINATION SKIN.

Your skin is usually oily in the T-zone (your forehead, nose, and chin, which form the shape of a "T") and dry on your cheeks. Take special care of it by using a gentle cleanser in the morning and at night. **If you use an astringent or toner, use it only on the oily parts.** Beauty companies now make moisturizers especially for combination skin like yours, but an oil-free moisturizer is a good bet, too.

The Do's
OF SKIN CARE

1. DO wash your face twice a day.

Use warm water and a gentle, unscented face wash in the morning and before you go to bed at night. (**Warm water helps open your pores so you can clean them more deeply.**) Wash by gently moving your fingertips or a washcloth in a circular motion over your skin—don't scrub hard! And don't forget often-missed places like the sides of your nose and just under your chin.

2. DO moisturize!

Don't be afraid to use moisturizer even if you have oily skin. Trying to strip all the oil from your face will dry out your pores, which causes them to produce more zit-causing oil to fight the dryness! Just **use a moisturizer designed for your skin type twice a day**—once in the morning and once at night—after washing your face.

3. DO exfoliate once a week.

"Exfoliate" is a fancy way of saying you're getting rid of dead skin that can build up and clog pores. You can exfoliate by using your regular cleanser with an exfoliating pad (sort of like a tiny loofah for your face) or with an exfoliating cleanser or scrub. Whichever you use, *be gentle!* Scrubbing too hard will irritate your skin, causing it to break out even more!

4. DO use the right products.

Make sure your moisturizer, concealer, and any makeup you wear are all labeled **"oil free," "noncomedogenic,"** or **"nonacnegenic."** (These are just fancy words that mean the product won't clog your pores or cause acne.)

5. DO keep hair off your face.

Be sure to keep your hair clean—or at least out of your face. If oily hair constantly brushes against your cheeks and forehead, acne may pop up there.

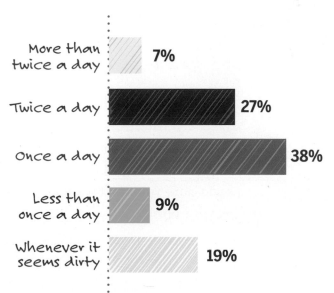

How often do you wash your face?

More than twice a day	7%
Twice a day	27%
Once a day	38%
Less than once a day	9%
Whenever it seems dirty	19%

The Don'ts
OF SKIN CARE

1. DON'T touch!

Keep your hands away from your face as much as possible! **Touching everyday things can cause germs to build up on your fingers,** and if those germs come in contact with your face, you're more likely to break out.

2. DON'T pop zits!

Popping or **picking at pimples can make them last longer** or cause infections and scars that are hard to get rid of.

3. DON'T wear makeup to bed.

If you use concealer to hide pimples— or wear any other makeup—make sure you **wash it off it before bed every single night.**

4. DON'T wait to wash your face.

After a workout or any time you've been sweating a lot, wash your face as soon as you can—**you don't want extra sweat and oil to clog your pores.**

80% of girls over age 8 have **problems with acne!**

Acne

Acne is a big deal. **It's hard not to be self-conscious when you have a zit on your face. You feel like everyone is looking at you, even when they're not.** Acne that doesn't clear up for weeks or months is even worse—it can damage your self-confidence and your self-esteem. **The good news? There are treatments that help clear up acne**...and we're here to help you find the ones that work for you.

·····Types of Acne Blemishes·····

Whiteheads are closed pores that have become clogged with oil and dead skin cells. A whitehead looks like a small bump with a white dot on the surface.

Blackheads are just like whiteheads, but the pores are open. This means all the stuff clogging the pore has been exposed to more air, which turns it black.

Cystic acne happens when clogged pores become infected and inflamed, causing red, painful bumps. For some people, cystic acne can get so bad it leaves scars if not treated.

How can I GET RID OF ACNE?

First, follow our handy-dandy skin care Do's and Don'ts. If a zit pops up, there's still hope! There are lots of products to help you fight and treat acne. **Because everyone's skin is different, you'll have to experiment to find the one that works best for you.** Be sure to follow the instructions on the package...using too much of these products can make acne way worse!

TIP

Many acne products contain an ingredient called benzoyl peroxide. It's great for fighting zits, but it'll bleach fabric. Make sure you wash it off your hands before touching your clothes!

What if my ACNE STILL WON'T GO AWAY?

If you've tried lots of products and nothing helps, **ask your parents if you can see a dermatologist—a doctor who specializes in skin problems.** Severe acne is serious—it can leave scars. You may need stronger treatments than the ones you can buy off the shelf in the store, or just a skin-care routine that's tailored to your needs. There are a lot of treatment options out there for you, so don't get discouraged. You'll find the right one—just don't give up!

You're probably going to break out now and then no matter *what* you do—**for most people, pimples are just part of growing up.** But remember, your skin problems seems worse to you than to anyone else, and most of your classmates are going through the same thing. **Almost everyone has experienced a couple of zits here and there. The best thing you can do is keep your skin clean and your chin up!**

> When I get a pimple, I always feel like everyone's staring at me. But then I remind myself that no one goes through puberty without getting pimples every once in a while. It's not as big as I think it is, and I can still smile and be confident when I have a pimple!"

6

Body Care

Body Care

Remember when keeping clean was all about playing in the tub with a couple of bath toys a few times a week? Now you worry about B.O., stinky feet, and even odors "down there." What happened? You're right—hormones happened! Thanks to them, your body needs more care than it did when you were a little kid. So let's talk about how to deal...

> *I used to only shower every other day unless I had soccer practice or something, but now I shower every day no matter what! Deodorant is good, but you have to stay clean, too.*

Body Odor

You *knew* we had to get to B.O. sometime, right? Just like your oil glands, **your sweat glands are working overtime during puberty.** Your underarms are loaded with sweat glands, and they're also two of the hottest parts on your body. When you sweat, the heat and moisture allow bacteria to grow—and *that's* what causes body odor. Gross, right?

> *I was in second grade and had early B.O. I hated wearing deodorant and always forgot to put it on. I'm in fifth grade now and I still forget to wear it, but after smelling the other kids in my class, I get it! Pee-eewww!*

Helpful Tips
BODY ODOR

Two of the most common products girls use to keep B.O. under control are deodorant and antiperspirant.

1. Deodorant

Your number one odor-busting tool comes in stick or gel form or in spray cans. **Deodorant works by killing the nasty bacteria that cause odor and by masking the smell with perfumes.** When you start to notice dampness or a funny odor in your underarms, ask your parents if you can start wearing deodorant. You might feel a little weird asking, but they'll understand!

TIP

Deodorant or antiperspirant that's labeled "invisible" won't leave white marks on your clothes.

Why did you start wearing deodorant?

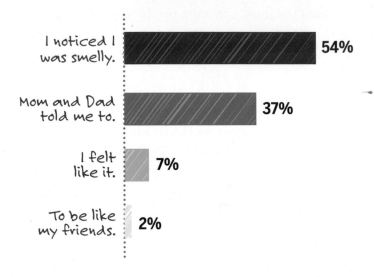

I noticed I was smelly. — **54%**

Mom and Dad told me to. — **37%**

I felt like it. — **7%**

To be like my friends. — **2%**

2. Antiperspirant

It's deodorant with a bonus—**antiperspirant reduces the amount you sweat.** If you want to keep your pits as dry as possible, antiperspirant is the way to go. On the other hand,

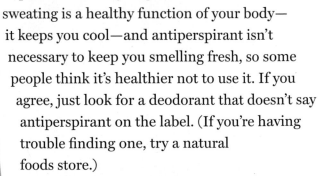

sweating is a healthy function of your body— it keeps you cool—and antiperspirant isn't necessary to keep you smelling fresh, so some people think it's healthier not to use it. If you agree, just look for a deodorant that doesn't say antiperspirant on the label. (If you're having trouble finding one, try a natural foods store.)

Once you start wearing deodorant or antiperspirant, make sure to keep it up every day! Your nose (and your classmates) will thank you!

"I was at my gymnastics practice, and *I noticed this awful smell* and realized it was me! It scared me a little, because it took us two months to find a deodorant I wasn't allergic to... but we finally did!"

"One day my mom casually mentioned that I smelled a little 'funky.' I felt stunned and hurt, but then I began to realize *I wasn't the only one.*"

"My mom and sister bought deodorant at the store and *told me I needed it.* It worried me because I wondered, 'Do I smell bad? How long has it been this way?'"

When did you start wearing deodorant?

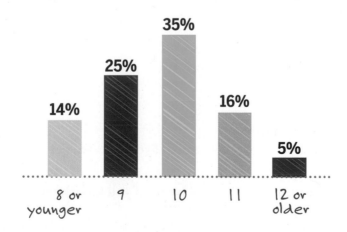

35% — 10
25% — 9
16% — 11
14% — 8 or younger
5% — 12 or older

Stinky Feet

You may notice that **your feet are sweating and stinking more,** too. You're not alone—have you ever been in the locker room after gym class when people are taking off their sneakers? You probably wished you had a pair of nose plugs!

What can I do about STINKY FEET?

1. Keep Clean

Wash your feet and dry them well, especially between the toes. Okay, that sounds obvious, but seriously— you need to get them *dry*. Remember, stinky bacteria love to grow in warm *damp* places.

2. Get Some Air

Loosen your laces and open up your shoes a bit to air them out overnight. Sprinkling in a little baking soda helps soak up the odor and dampness, too.

3. Don't Go Bare

Wear socks with sneakers. Cotton socks are best—they absorb sweat better.

4. Mix It Up

Switch shoes every day or two if you can. We get that some shoes are so cute you want to wear them every day, but they'll smell better if you give them time to air out!

"Once I was playing truth or dare with
my friends, and somebody had to
choose who had the stinkiest feet. They
chose mine! I was mortified!"

Take Care
(Down There...)

Your private parts don't come with an owner's manual—well, now you have this one! **Let's talk about how you can keep them clean and healthy.**

You may notice new odors coming from down there, especially when you're on your period, but there's no reason to worry—it's normal and healthy. As long as you **wash between your legs with mild soap and water and put on clean cotton underwear every day,** odor shouldn't be a problem. (Make sure to change out of a damp bathing suit or sweaty leotard as soon as you can, too!) And save the scented body washes for the rest of your body, not your private parts—you don't want to irritate that sensitive skin.

TIP

The first step to keeping clean (down there) is changing your underwear every day!

I've heard you can GET INFECTIONS DOWN THERE. What are they?

Two of the most common types of infections girls and women get are yeast infections and urinary tract infections (UTIs).

1. Yeast infection: Even a healthy vagina has some yeast in it, but sometimes too much yeast grows, and then you get itching, burning, pain when you pee, and an abnormal discharge that looks a bit like cottage cheese. Yeast infections are pretty common, but they're usually very easy to treat. So **if you start to feel itchy down there and have an unusual discharge, talk to your mom or your doctor.** You don't have to suffer through it!

2. UTI: A UTI happens when bacteria start to grow somewhere in your urinary tract—the part of your body that deals with your pee. It hurts or burns when you pee, and you might get a fever. You might also feel like you have to pee often, but when you try, very little comes out. Some girls even get stomachaches or feel nauseous. **If it ever hurts to pee or you think you might have a UTI, tell your mom or dad.** UTIs can be serious if left untreated, but luckily, they're usually easy to treat with medicine from your doctor.

The best ways to prevent UTIs are to **drink lots of water and have good bathroom habits.** Which brings us to…

*Source: WomensHealth.gov

Helpful Tips
BATHROOM HYGIENE

1. Don't hold it in.
If you feel like you need to pee, do it as soon as you can, and definitely before you become uncomfortable. Holding your pee in for a long time can lead to a urinary tract infection.

2. Moist wipes are your friend!
If you have moist wipes in your bathroom, it's a good idea to use them, especially after you poop—they'll make you feel cleaner than plain toilet paper.

3. Wipe from front to back.
After using the bathroom (no matter what you do in there), wipe with toilet paper from front to back—not the other way around. If you wipe from back to front, you risk bacteria from your anus getting into your urethra or your vagina, which can lead to infections. And you don't want those!

4. Wash your hands!
We know you've heard this before, but washing your hands is really important after you use the restroom (especially if it's a public restroom). You don't want to spread germs around to everybody else!

Body Hair & Shaving

It's funny—you probably don't even give a second thought to hair in some places (like your head), but in others, it gives you a total shock! If you're weirded out, don't be! **Everybody gets hair in new places as they go through puberty, and it's totally natural and normal.** For a lot of girls, growing hair where you used to have none is one of the first signs that you're starting puberty—it can happen before you start growing breasts, get your period, or even hit a growth spurt.

As we mentioned earlier, you'll get new hair around your privates (called pubic hair) and in your underarms during puberty. **This new hair will grow gradually, starting out sparse and light but getting thicker and darker as you get older.** The color of your new body hair will depend on a lot of things, but it will most likely be a **shade or two darker than the hair on your head.** And sometimes, blonde girls grow underarm hair or pubic hair that's brown.

The most important thing to know about body hair is that it's completely normal and natural. Many girls feel that having body hair, especially under their arms and on their legs, isn't girly or cool as they enter middle school. If all the girls in your class are starting to shave their legs, you might feel pressured to, too. But **don't let others push you into doing something before you're ready.** It's a very personal decision. You don't have to do anything at all about your new body hair, but if you're interested in removing it, you do have options.

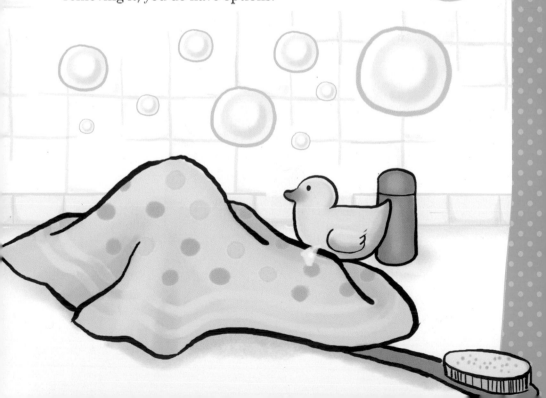

WHAT DO I NEED TO KNOW before I start shaving?

Before you do anything, talk to an adult. Hair removal treatments can irritate, burn, or cut your skin. (You don't want to end up looking like the cat attacked your leg!) **When you're ready to start shaving, your mom (or even your dad) can be a great resource, so be sure to let them help you.**

When it comes to the hair between your legs, keep in mind that no one but you will see that part of your body anyway. As you get older and the hair gets thicker, some of it may show when you're wearing a swimsuit and make you self-conscious. A lot of older girls shave that little bit of hair (often called the "bikini area"). If you choose to do so, too, be extra careful using a razor around that delicate area!

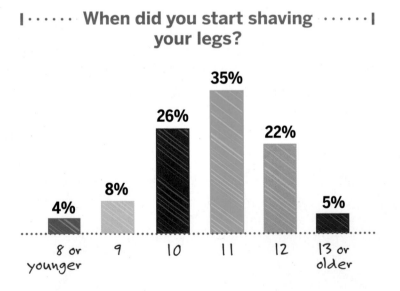

When did you start shaving your legs?

- 8 or younger: 4%
- 9: 8%
- 10: 26%
- 11: 35%
- 12: 22%
- 13 or older: 5%

"*I was really nervous!* I was like, 'Come on, shave,' and then I was like, 'No, what if you cut yourself?!' I got over it and just did it, and after, my legs were silky smooth."

"I didn't know what to do, so I just shaved my legs dry with a razor and *it hurt so bad!*"

"*I wish I would have waited longer.* I just got pressured into it by my friends who shave."

"I just wanted to shave because my best friend did it. And I'm bored with it already! *It takes too much time* and it is a pain in the neck."

"I used to have really thick dark hair all over my legs. I always got made fun of and *people called me 'Sasquatch.'* I hated it, so I asked my mom if I could start shaving."

"I asked my mom three times if I could shave, and she said no. I gave up and figured I have blonde hair, so what does it matter? Then one day, she gave me a razor. *Just be patient; it's not a big deal.*"

Helpful Tips
ON SHAVING

1. Shave When Wet

Never shave dry skin. Always use water plus soap or shaving gel so your skin doesn't get irritated. (Most girls shave in the shower.)

2. Shave Up the Leg

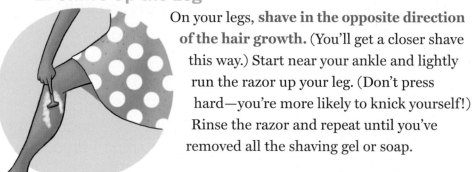

On your legs, **shave in the opposite direction of the hair growth.** (You'll get a closer shave this way.) Start near your ankle and lightly run the razor up your leg. (Don't press hard—you're more likely to knick yourself!) Rinse the razor and repeat until you've removed all the shaving gel or soap.

3. Shave Knees Carefully

To shave your knees, pull the skin tight and go slow. You're less likely to cut yourself that way.

4. Shave Underarms Both Ways

The hair in your underarms grows in several directions, so shave up and down, left and right—it's the best way to get a close shave.

5. Shave Lightly

Shaving can sometimes cause ingrown hairs. **This happens when a hair grows back into your skin,** creating a red bump, like a miniature pimple. (Yeah...like you need another pimple!) Shaving lightly will lessen the chances of getting an ingrown hair, but if you do, **you can treat it with a special cream** or ask your mom or dad to lift the end of the hair out using tweezers.

6. Keep Your Razor Clean

Rinse your razor well when you're done, and let it air dry. Also, remember to change your razor blade on a regular basis, usually after five shaves. Dull razors can lead to more cuts...the last thing you want!

DID YOU KNOW?

Shaving does not make hair grow back faster and thicker—even though many people think it does. Hair only seems thicker because it's dull at the ends after being cut by a razor.

Choosing to shave (and even when to wear deodorant) is a very personal decision. Just because your friends are doing these things doesn't mean that you need to. You're in charge of your body. **Trust yourself to know when it's the right time for you.**

> *I don't mind some of the changes. Wearing deodorant made me feel more grown up, and I was so-o-o happy when my mom finally said I could shave my legs.*

7

Loving Yourself

> How you feel about yourself shapes you and how others see you. People are drawn to you when you feel comfortable in your own skin. Loving yourself is so important!

Body Image

Do you love everything about the way you look?
If your immediate answer is no, you're hardly alone.
You're surrounded by seemingly perfect-looking girls
on TV shows, in movies, and in advertisements for
clothes and products. At school, you're super aware
of those girls who seem to have skipped any sign of
an awkward stage **(not fair!).**

To top it off, **your body is going through changes
that you can't control,** just when you feel like
you're in the middle of a perfect storm of pressure to
look a certain way. It's no wonder so many girls end
up staring in their mirrors, studying every aspect of
their looks...

How we feel about our looks is called our body image—it's part of
our overall self-esteem (how we feel about ourselves in general).
**Self-esteem is important. Why? Because feeling good about
yourself can affect how you act.** A girl who has high self-esteem
will make friends easily, be more in control of her behavior, and
enjoy life more.

When we asked girls what they were most insecure about, most mentioned their physical appearance. A few wrote things like "I'm too shy" or "I can't sing," but the overwhelming majority listed a *physical* feature. "I feel like I'm fat." "I'm way too skinny." "I'm too tall." "I'm too short." "I hate my nose, my skin, my hair, my flat chest...!" All the negative body talk was enough to make anyone feel down.

DID YOU KNOW?

50% of girls say that they feel their **bodies are not the "right" size.**

33% of girls say they have already been on a **diet.**

30% of girls say their biggest insecurity is that they're **not pretty enough.**

But there's good news, too. **You don't have to live with a bad body image**—and the sooner you work on changing your thinking and loving yourself, the happier you'll be!

A lot of girls at school are prettier than me. How can I STOP COMPARING myself to them?

With all the pressure to look perfect, it can be a challenge to love yourself the way you are. And it can be especially hard to feel great about your body when it's going through a ton of changes. **Every** girl—no matter how perfect she seems—feels awkward and less than perfect at some point during puberty. You are so not alone!

Here's the problem with comparing yourself to other people: no matter what, you'll always find someone who's "better" than you. If you focus on what's so great about her, you'll lose sight of what's great about you. All that comparing is like a bad habit—the more you think about it, the harder it is to *stop* thinking about it.

I wish I looked like her!

That's not to say that it's a bad thing to want to change, though. If your hair is hard to manage, ask your hairdresser how to tame it, or look up tips on the Internet. If you want to get into better shape, find a fun way to get moving. **Making an effort to look and feel your best is a way of loving yourself and your body, too.** Learning to do your hair or dress in a cute, flattering way isn't just about looks—it's a way of taking back a sense of power and control over your own body! You'll feel more confident about what you see in the mirror, and boost your self-esteem, too.

> *Everybody is different, so if we are constantly comparing ourselves to others, we will always be faced with disappointment. A lot of girls at my school are always saying they wish they were like this one really pretty girl. I think it's dumb. Comparing just brings you down because you will never be that person.*

How can I feel good when I CAN'T CHANGE the things I don't like about myself?

The truth is that nobody will ever be completely, 100 percent satisfied with themselves. And that's fine—every girl has her imperfections, and that's what makes her totally unique. This is the body that you were born with, so why would you want to spend your life worrying about your "flaws"? Besides, how boring would life be if everyone looked the same?

Ultimately, the only person who can quiet your negative thoughts is *you*. You know what we mean...that voice whispering that your hair is too frizzy, your feet are too big, or your nose is too pointy. Sure, we all have our insecurities, but we bet there are also tons of things you like about yourself. The next time you start thinking that you're not good enough, **write down the things you *do* love about yourself—both physical and non-physical**—like your big hazel eyes, your athletic ability, and your kindness. Before long, you won't have any room left for negative thoughts—you'll be too busy thinking positive ones instead!

66% of girls say someone's mean comment has made them **feel bad about themselves.**

I try to love myself, but sometimes PEOPLE SAY MEAN THINGS and it gets to me.

If a girl at school says, "You look fat in those jeans," you can either start to worry about the size of your rear end, or you can tell yourself there's no reason you should accept her opinion of you. Chances are, the comment has very little to do with you anyway—**the person who said it was probably just trying to tear you down because she felt bad about herself.** Besides, who says *she* gets to decide what looks good? What's beautiful to one person might not be to another—and vice versa. Why give other people power over something as important as how you feel about your own body?

> *In fourth grade, I was bullied because I was a little bit bigger than the other girls. I was not fat, I was just built different, but I started to believe them, and every day my confidence went down. But after a while I thought, why did I believe them? Just because your body is different does not mean it isn't beautiful.*

When you come right down to it, it's confidence—not looks— that people are drawn to (and become jealous of). Even if you're insecure, make a point of *acting* confident. You might have to fake it a little at first, but trust us—it works! If you carry yourself like you truly love and value yourself, you'll soon start to feel that way for real. You owe it to yourself to embrace the girl in the mirror, and there's no better time to start than now!

What Girls Say...
They Love About Their Bodies

"**I love everything** about my body! The changes make me feel sooo beautiful!"

"I like **the way my clothes fit** now that I've started getting curves."

"I'm taller, and I'm very proud of it. I have **great legs for running**, pedaling on my bike, and jumping to spike the ball in volleyball!"

"Being a gymnast, I am aware of my power. I am proud of my body because **it does hard things**."

138

But stars look PERFECT, so why can't I?

You know those images you see of actresses and models with perfect skin and super-skinny bodies? They're not true to life. Makeup and technology allow real-looking people to become perfect-looking photos. Plus, celebrities have teams of stylists and makeup artists swarming around them at all times, making very real flaws nearly invisible.

It can be hard not to compare yourself to celebrities—their faces are everywhere! But when you expect to look like a star, you are being incredibly unfair to yourself.

VIPFLASH

On the next two pages, we'll show you just what goes into making those "perfect" photos.

> *I know a lot of girls who compare themselves to famous people. My friends feel like they aren't good enough the way they are. I wish they could use stars as inspiration to keep practicing and working harder at their own talents instead of wishing they looked like them.*

Is She for Real?
CREATING THE PERFECT IMAGE

Meet Catherine, a 12-year-old *Discovery Girls* reader, who agreed to be our model for a day so that we could show you what goes into creating the perfect magazine cover.

A Makeover

Just like a celebrity, Catherine spent hours with our professional makeup artists and hairstylists, getting a complete makeover.

Hair Extensions

We used makeup to make her features more dramatic and glued on hair extensions to give her long, curly locks.

Posing for Photos

Then, Catherine posed for hundreds of photos. Yes, it takes that many just to get a few good ones! We chose the best photo... and then our photo editors got to work.

Digital Editing

Through the magic of digital editing, we took Catherine's photo from great to "perfect"! We even changed her dress for a more dramatic style!

The Magic of Digital Editing

Before ⋯⋯⋯⋯⋯⋯⋯⋯⋯⋯⋯⋯⋯⋯⋯⋯⋯ After

Made her taller ⋯⋯⋯⋯⋯

Added more eye makeup ⋯⋯⋯⋯

Darkened hair ⋯⋯⋯

Evened out skin tone ⋯⋯⋯⋯

Removed jewelry ⋯⋯

Changed dress ⋯⋯

Changed shoe color ⋯⋯

We turned Catherine into a glamorous cover model just to show you how it's done. But when you think about it, being a real-life cover girl probably isn't a self-esteem booster, even for a celebrity! No one, no matter how pretty she is, could feel great about how she looks on a magazine cover when it takes so much work by so many people to create that illusion of perfection. Think about it: If your image had to be changed so much you hardly recognized yourself, how beautiful would *you* feel?

(And just so you know...at *Discovery Girls* magazine, we don't alter girls' photos like this. We believe every girl is unique and special just as she is.)

Those negative thoughts always come back. How can I get rid of them for good?

No matter how committed you are to loving yourself, it's not something that happens overnight. Even after weeks or months, the thoughts that you're not good enough might still come back to get you down. That's actually okay. Part of accepting yourself is accepting that you won't feel good about yourself a hundred percent of the time. When those thoughts start up again—and you start feeling insecure—just remind yourself that you're not thinking like that anymore. **Every time mean thoughts pop up, replace them with positive ones.** It'll take time, but if you keep at it, you'll hear them less and less.

Remember, you're the only person in the world who can give you a good body image. You can choose to beat yourself up for not being born with the genes of a supermodel...or you can **choose to flood your brain with so many positive thoughts** there's no room left for negative ones. You can waste your time and energy wishing you were something you're not, or you can love yourself—imperfections and all—and be the best possible *you*. **In the end, it's up to you. Which do you choose?**

> *A couple of years ago, I realized that the girls who were considered the most 'pretty' in my school were the most confident. They didn't look like super-models—they were just normal girls who smiled and weren't insecure.*

Glossary

Confused by all those new puberty words?
Here's what they mean!

Acne: a skin condition that shows up as bumps on your face, shoulders, upper back, and chest. Also called "pimples" or "zits."

Antiperspirant: a product you put on your underarms that reduces the amount you sweat.

Anus: the hole where your poop comes out.

Areola: the darker skin surrounding your nipple. It can be any color from pink to light brown to dark brown, and you might have little bumps or hairs on it.

Astringent: a facial product that kills bacteria and helps oily skin.

Band size: how big a bra is around your chest and back, represented by the number in a bra size.

Benzoyl peroxide: an ingredient in pimple creams and gels that treats acne.

Bikini area: the pubic hair on your inner thighs that shows when you're wearing a swimsuit.

Blackhead: an open pore that is clogged with oil and dead skin cells. Being open to the air is what turns a blackhead black.

Body image: how you feel about your physical appearance.

Breast bud: the nickel-sized bump that starts to stick out under your nipple in the second stage of breast development. Growing breast buds is called "budding."

Breast tenderness: soreness in your breasts or nipples that you might get during or right before your period.

Cami: an undershirt with thin straps that some girls wear for extra coverage before they are ready for a bra. Cami is short for "camisole."

Clitoris: a sensitive spot in your vulva that may feel good to the touch but doesn't serve any other function.

Combination skin: skin that is dry in some places and oily in others.

Cramps: pains in your tummy area, lower back, or upper thighs that are caused by the muscles of your uterus squeezing during your period.

Cup size: the size of your actual breast, represented by the letter in a bra size.

Cystic acne: clogged pores that become infected and inflamed, causing red, painful bumps.

Deodorant: a product that you put on your underarms to kill bacteria and mask body odor with perfumes.

Depression: a serious condition that makes you feel sad and hopeless all the time for two weeks or longer.

Dermatologist: a doctor who specializes in skin problems. A dermatologist can help treat your acne.

Endorphins: chemicals in your body that make you feel happy. Your brain makes endorphins when you exercise, laugh, or smile.

Estrogen: the hormone that girls have more of that makes you develop curves and breasts, controls your period, and sometimes messes with your emotions.

Exfoliate: to get rid of dead skin on your face that can clog pores and cause acne.

Facial cleanser: a special soap made just for washing your face.

Fallopian tubes: the parts inside your body that carry the ova, or eggs, from your ovaries to your uterus.

Fashion bra: a bra for girls who are a little more developed. It is sometimes called an "underwire bra."

Flow: how much blood comes out during your period. Some days you'll have a heavier flow and other days you'll have a lighter flow.

Growing pains: aches in your lower legs that sometimes happen when you're going through a growth spurt.

Growth spurt: growing a lot taller in a short period of time.

Hormones: chemicals your body makes to help it function and grow.

Ingrown hair: hair that grows back into your skin after you shave.

Labia: "lips" that protect the delicate parts inside your vulva. They look slightly different on every girl.

Menstrual cycle: the time from the start of one period to the start of the next one. A normal menstrual cycle can be anywhere from 21 to 45 days.

Menstruation: the fancy medical word for your period.

Moisturizer: a special facial lotion that keeps your skin from being too dry.

Nonacnegenic: a fancy way to say "won't cause acne."

Noncomedogenic: a fancy way to say "won't clog pores."

Ova: the eggs your ovaries produce that will develop into a baby if you decide to get pregnant one day.

Ovaries: the parts inside your body that produce ova, or eggs.

Overnight pad: an extra-long, thick pad designed for you to wear while you sleep.

Pad: a cotton-like material that sticks to your underwear to soak up your period blood. Pads are also called maxi pads, sanitary pads, or sanitary napkins.

Panty liner: a small, extra-thin pad that's perfect for days when you have barely any flow, or for extra protection when you're wearing a tampon.

Period: the time each month when blood comes out of your vagina for about 3 to 5 days. Most girls have their first period at age 11 or 12.

Pores: tiny holes in your skin where oil comes out.

Puberty: the time when your body matures from a child's body into an adult body. It can start anywhere from age 8 to 14 and lasts 3 to 5 years.

Pubic hair: body hair that grows around your private parts and inner thighs.

Salicylic acid: an ingredient in pimple creams and gels that treats acne.

Sebum: oil your skin produces to lubricate your skin and hair. If your pores become clogged with too much sebum, you can get acne.

Self-esteem: how you feel about yourself in general. Your self-esteem can affect how you act.

Shaving gel: a special gel or cream made to protect your skin when you shave.

Sports bra: a super supportive bra with wider straps that's designed for sports.

Sweat glands: glands under your skin that make sweat. You have a lot of them in your underarms and on your feet.

Tampon: a bit of cotton-like material that you insert into your vagina to soak up your period blood.

Testosterone: the hormone that boys have more of that makes them grow facial hair and get deeper voices, and that sometimes messes with their emotions, too.

Toner: a facial product that cleans your skin and makes your pores look smaller.

Toxic Shock Syndrome (TSS): an extremely rare but very serious disease that happens when bacteria become toxic to your body. It can be caused by wearing a tampon too long.

Training bra: a stretchy, comfy bra that gets you used to wearing bras.

T-zone: your forehead, nose, and chin, which form the shape of a "T."

Urethra: the hole in your vulva where your pee comes out.

Urinary tract infection (UTI): an infection in your urinary tract—the part of your body that deals with your pee—caused by bacteria.

Uterus: the part inside your body where a baby will grow if you ever decide to get pregnant. Your period blood comes from your uterus.

Vagina: the part of your vulva where your period blood comes out.

Vaginal discharge: a clear or white fluid about the thickness of mucus that comes out of your vagina to flush out bad bacteria.

Vulva: the whole area of your private parts around your vagina, including the labia, clitoris, and urethra.

Whitehead: a closed pore that is clogged with oil and dead skin cells. A whitehead looks like a small bump with a white dot on top.

Yeast infection: an infection caused by too much yeast in your vagina. A yeast infection itches, makes it hurt when you pee, and causes a cottage cheese-like discharge.

Why Are Friendships So Confusing?

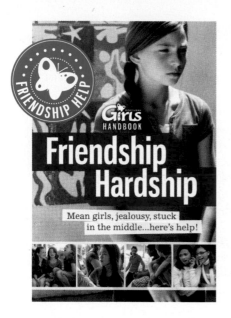

SHE KNOWS EVERYTHING about you...she'd never tell your secrets... she's your biggest fan. Who doesn't want a friend like that?

True friendship is a gift...but it can be hard to find. Whether you're stuck in a fading friendship, caught in the popularity trap, or dealing with mean girls, we'll break down the solutions to your problems step by step. Best of all, we'll teach you how to free yourself from poisonous friendships forever and be the best friend you can be.

Soon, you'll be meeting new people and making friends who truly respect and understand you...because you deserve first-rate friendships.

Getting Unstuck

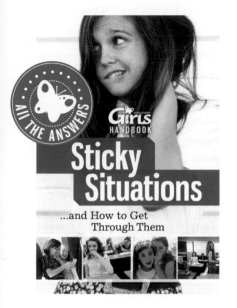

REMEMBER WHEN YOU got up the courage to tell your crush you liked him...and found out he didn't like you back? Didn't you wish you knew someone who had all the answers?

Well, have no fear! Not only do we know exactly how to handle your crush (what is wrong with him, anyway?), but we also know how to deal with a gazillion other sticky situations. Like when your BFF blabs your deepest secret to the entire school...or when you make a total fool of yourself onstage.

We'll also tell you how to handle being bullied by mean girls...or stranded at the mall...and much, much more! By the last page, you'll be ready to deal with anything!

Look for this and other bestselling titles at DiscoveryGirls.com
ISBN 978-1-934766-05-7
$9.95

When Did Life Get So Complicated?

STUCK BETWEEN FRIENDS?
Tired of your siblings? Self-conscious about your body? Crushing big time?

You're not alone. Every month, girls write to *Discovery Girls* magazine to ask Ali, our advice columnist, for help with issues like these.

When it comes to girls' most troublesome questions, Ali has all the answers you need. She tackles your questions on everything from family to friendship to school to boys...and much, much more.

No matter what you're going through, you'll find answers to your problems inside. Ali is here to help!

Look for this and other bestselling titles at DiscoveryGirls.com
ISBN 978-1-934766-10-1
$9.95

Getting Over Bad Days

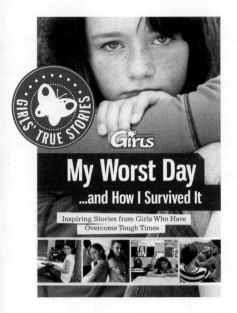

AUBRIE'S BEST FRIEND told her they couldn't be friends anymore because Aubrie was "too weird" to be seen with. Torrie was so upset when her parents divorced, she gained 20 pounds and let her grades go into freefall. Mackenzie watched her mom grow sicker and sicker and then die, just when Mackenzie needed her most.

In these amazing true stories, girls just like you share their private struggles, hoping to help you through your most difficult times.

You'll find comfort, encouragement, and inspiration here...and best of all, you'll know that whatever life throws at you, you are never alone.

Look for this and other bestselling titles at DiscoveryGirls.com
ISBN 978-1-934766-07-1
$9.95